DOES THE PREACHER BELIEVE WHAT THEY PREACH?

Meosha Culpepper

Does The Preacher Believe What They Preach?

© **2025 by Meosha Culpepper**
All rights reserved.

No part of this publication may be reproduced, distributed, or transmitted in any form or by any means, including photocopying, recording, scanning, or any other electronic or mechanical methods, without the prior written permission of the publisher, except in the case of brief quotations embodied in critical reviews, articles, or other noncommercial uses permitted by copyright law.

Scripture quotations, unless otherwise noted, are taken from the Holy Bible, King James Version. Public domain.

This book is a work of nonfiction. Some names and identifying details may have been changed to protect the privacy of individuals. Any resemblance to actual persons, living or deceased, or actual events is purely coincidental.

Published by: BUT GOD Publishings LLC

Printed in the United States of America.

For permissions, inquiries, or author contact, please visit: www.terministries.com

DEDICATION

This book is dedicated to every believer who ever sat in a sanctuary with silent pain. To every servant who gave their heart to ministry and was left wounded. To every voice that was silenced for speaking truth, and to every soul who questioned God because of what people did in His name.

May these pages remind you that God sees you,
God knows you,
God hears you,
and God has never confused the actions of man with the purity of your heart.

I also dedicate this book to the next generation of leaders: those who dare to preach with integrity,
lead with humility,
love with compassion,
and walk in holiness.

May you become the shepherds after God's own heart that this world desperately needs.

And lastly, to the younger version of myself:
thank you for surviving,
thank you for holding on,
and thank you for never letting the fire inside you die.

This book is the fruit of your endurance.

ACKNOWLEDGMENTS

As I reflect on the journey that led to this book, my heart is full of gratitude. This book was not written in isolation; it was written through life, through pain, through growth, through healing, and through the endless grace of God. I want to honor the people, moments, and spiritual encounters that carried me to this point.

First and foremost, **to my Heavenly Father**. Thank You Jesus for being my anchor, my truth, my healer, and my Shepherd. Thank You for guiding me through seasons I did not understand and for never leaving me alone in the storm. Your presence covered me when people failed me, Your voice guided me when leadership misled me, and Your love restored me when ministry wounded me. This book exists because You sustained me.

To **every person who survived spiritual abuse**, who lost their voice but found it again, who walked away from a building but not from God. Thank you. Your courage inspired me. Your stories reminded me that I was not alone. And your pain strengthened my resolve to write with honesty and boldness. This book is for you.

To **my family**, thank you for loving me, supporting me, and standing with me through the highs and lows. Your presence helped me feel grounded when life felt unstable. Your encouragement helped me keep moving forward when I wanted to give up.

To **my true friends! The ones who prayed, checked in, listened, and held space for my healing**, thank you. You honored my journey without judgment. You covered me when I couldn't cover myself. You held my heart with compassion and handled my truth with care.

To **those God strategically placed in my path during the hardest seasons**; my mentors, counselors, professors, spiritual encouragers, and the unexpected voices who spoke life at just the right time. You may never know how much your words meant to me. God used you as reminders that purity still exists, that truth still matters, and that He still raises up leaders who reflect His heart.

To **the individuals who unintentionally pushed me toward my purpose**. Those who mishandled me, underestimated me, or tried to silence me; thank you as well. You taught me what kind of leader I will never be. You sharpened my discernment, strengthened my voice, and pushed me closer to God. You played a role in shaping the ministry I walk in today.

To **every reader holding this book**, thank you for your openness, your courage, and your willingness to confront truth. My prayer is that these pages bring clarity, healing, and a fresh encounter with God. May you feel seen, strengthened, and spiritually awakened.

And finally, to **the younger version of me**; the one who didn't understand why she had to walk through what she walked through. Thank you for surviving. Thank you for holding on. Thank you for not giving up. Every tear you cried became oil for this moment. Every wound you endured became wisdom for this assignment. You didn't know it then, but God was writing this book through you all along.

To everyone mentioned and everyone who walks this journey with me, **thank you**. Your presence, prayers, and love helped birth this book.

To God be the glory!

AUTHOR'S NOTE

There are certain books you choose to write, and then there are books that choose you.

This is one of the latter.

I did not wake up one day with a desire to confront spiritual abuse, hypocrisy, or corruption in the church. I did not volunteer to expose experiences that still carry emotional weight. I did not seek out the responsibility of addressing what many believers suffer silently.

But God assigned me this book long before I understood why.

For years, I held my questions privately.
For years, I carried wounds quietly.
For years, I tried to protect the very leaders who harmed me.
For years, I kept the truth buried so the church could remain comfortable.

But comfort does not produce healing.
Silence does not produce freedom.
And secrets do not produce holiness.

Writing this book required honesty with myself, with God, and with the Body of Christ. It required confronting realities that were painful to relive. It required walking through memories that shaped my discernment, my boundaries, and my calling. It required courage I didn't always feel I had.

But more than anything, writing this book required **obedience**.

Because this is not a book about tearing down the Church; it is a book about returning her to the heart of God.

This book is for the wounded, the overlooked, the faithful servants who gave everything to ministry only to be mishandled by those entrusted with their spiritual care. It is for those who have walked away from the building but not from God. It is for those who still believe in holiness, purity, and righteousness, even when leadership fails to model it.

This book is also for preachers.
For the leaders.
For the ones called to shepherd God's people.

It is a reminder that titles do not exempt us from accountability. That charisma is not a substitute for character. That God does not measure ministry by applause, but by obedience.
And that the pulpit is not a platform. It is a place of death to flesh.

I wrote this book because I am no longer afraid to tell the truth. I wrote it because too many believers are living in confusion and condemnation caused by leaders who refuse to live what they preach.
I wrote it because I survived it, and survived people rarely stay silent.
I wrote it because someone needs to know they are not alone. I wrote it because God told me there would be freedom in these pages.
And I wrote it because the Church is in a season of purification, and truth is part of that cleansing.

If anything in this book stirs you, challenges you, convicts you, or confirms something inside you; let it.
If anything in these pages resurrects wounds you tried to bury, allow God to heal them.

If anything brings clarity to questions you were too afraid to ask; receive it.

And if anything calls you higher; answer it.

This book is not the whole conversation, but it is the beginning of one.

I appreciate you taking the time to read with an open mind. Thank you for allowing my testimony to sit beside your own. Thank you for letting God speak to you through these words.

May truth set you free,
may healing find you,
and may God reveal Himself to you in ways no preacher ever could.

— **Meosha Culpepper**

"For nothing is hidden that will not be revealed, nor anything secret that will not be known." — Luke 12:2

"When truth rises, it does not rise to destroy the Church; it rises to cleanse her. May every preacher live what they declare, and may every believer see God beyond the ones who speak for Him."

INTRODUCTION

When the Messenger and the Message Don't Match

There comes a moment in every believer's life when the questions you've buried rise to the surface. Questions you never thought you would ask. Questions that seem risky. Questions that carry weight... Questions that feel like betrayal just for thinking them.

But there is one question that changed everything in my life:

Does the preacher believe what they preach?

This is not a question born out of rebellion.
It is not rooted in bitterness.
It is not fueled by hate.
It is birthed out of pain, and pain tells the truth.

I didn't start my journey suspicious of the church.
I started it with passion, purity, and hunger.
I loved God.
I loved His people.
I loved ministry.
And when I stepped into leadership, all I wanted was to serve Him with my whole heart.

But somewhere along the way, I witnessed things I never expected to see in a place that was supposed to be safe.
I saw the Word preached with fire and lived with hypocrisy.
I saw pulpits filled with charisma but empty of character.
I saw leaders who could prophesy with accuracy but lacked integrity.

I saw gifts celebrated while souls were neglected.
I saw manipulation wrapped in scripture and control disguised as "spiritual order."
And worst of all, I saw people wounded by the very ones called to shepherd them.

This book is not written to destroy the Church.
It is written to **heal her**.

It is not written to shame leaders.
It is written to **call them higher**.

It is not written to expose people.
It is written to **expose patterns**.
Systems.
Behaviors.
Mindsets.
Spirits that operate behind the scenes while the congregation lifts their hands unaware.

You may find yourself in these pages; not as a critic, but as someone who has lived through the confusion of witnessing a preacher declare one thing publicly while living another privately.
You may recognize wounds you buried, questions you silenced, or memories you tried to forget.
You may find your voice again.
You may find your healing again.
You may find your clarity again.

Because what I learned is this:

God can handle your questions, and He can handle your truth.

This book is the truth I wish someone had told me sooner. It is the truth many believers are afraid to say out loud. It is the truth that brings freedom, not shame.

I am not writing from a place of anger.
I am writing from a place of awakening.
A space for healing.

A space for renewal.
A place of boldness that only comes from surviving what was meant to silence me.

This book is for:

- those who were wounded in the pews

- those who served faithfully and were overlooked

- those who loved ministry but were mishandled by leadership

- those questioning their faith because of what they witnessed

- those who want truth, not theatrics

- those who believe holiness still matters

- those who know God is calling His church back to purity

If you have ever asked, "Is this really God?"
If you have ever felt betrayed by spiritual authority…
If you have ever walked away from church wondering if God walked away from you…
If you have ever watched a preacher preach one thing and live another…
This book will meet you right where you are.

I am not here to tear down the Church; I am here to tear down the lies that have held her hostage.

And as you read, I ask you to open your heart.
Not to the institution, but to God.

Not to tradition, but to truth.
Not to performance, but to purity.

Because when the dust settles, and when the noise fades, and when the masks fall…

The question that remains is the only one that truly matters:

Preacher, do you believe what you preach?

And just as important:
Believer, do you know the God behind the sermon?

Welcome to the journey.
Let the healing begin.
Let the awakening begin.
And let the truth be told.

TABLE OF CONTENTS

Does the Preacher Believe What They Preach?
By Meosha Culpepper

Chapter 1

The Call Before the Calling

I knew I was being pulled into something greater, but I didn't fully understand what it was. On the day of my ordination, I felt the atmosphere shift. In the spirit, I saw doors opening—multiple doors—but I didn't know what was behind any of them. All I knew was that God was calling me into a purpose that had been ordained before the foundations of the world.

But what people didn't see was the warfare that led up to that moment. It was horrific. Every attack felt personal. The pressure intensified with every day that I drew closer to ordination, and the enemy fought me with a force I had never experienced before. And yet, the more intense the battle became, the more I knew it was confirmation that God Himself was calling me. Hell doesn't fight what it doesn't fear.

My expectations of leadership were simple and pure. I believed ministry was about healing the sick, raising the dead, opening blind eyes—walking in power and carrying the weight of God's glory with discipline and dedication. I expected leadership to be rooted in servanthood, humility, and sacrifice.

But the reality was different.

Those over me made it hard to operate in what I knew God was telling me to do. Instead of support, I encountered resistance. Instead of nurturing, I met blockages. Instead of covering, I ran into defenses. Yet even in the frustration, I persevered. Every door they tried to close, God opened another one. Every time they pushed me to the side, God pushed me forward. Every time they tried to silence me, the Lord made my assignment louder.

But nothing prepared me for the moment when I realized that what I was seeing in the pulpit didn't match what I was witnessing in private.

When the Pulpit Doesn't Match the Person

One year during our annual church family and fun day at the beach, one of the leaders—who had already been making inappropriate advances toward me—invited me to a nearby bar and grill. I arrived expecting fellowship and food. Instead, I walked into a scene I will never forget.

There they were: my pastor, that leader, and another church member—drunk, stumbling, laughing, and enjoying themselves like it was a Saturday night in the club.

I was shocked, but not judgmental. I approached them with kindness, thinking I was walking in love. Instead, the pastor I once admired turned on me like an enemy. He cussed me out—publicly, loudly, and aggressively. The words stung deeper than any attack from the world ever could.

In that moment, a part of me shattered...

I was trying to live holy, trying to follow God, trying to honor leadership—and here I was standing in a bar watching the same man who preached holiness on Sunday cuss me out with alcohol on his breath.

I didn't just lose respect—I nearly lost my faith.

I had unknowingly placed him on a pedestal. I had idolized his anointing, thinking he could do no wrong. God had to expose the truth:
I was seeing him through spiritual blindness, not spiritual discernment.

That day was my awakening. From that moment on, I could tell when he was under the influence—even while preaching. The pulpit no longer felt pure. The sanctuary no longer felt safe.

And I began to question everything.

When Your Gift Matters More Than Your Soul

During a season of deep grief—when your childhood friend was dying—no one in leadership showed compassion. Not one checked on your heart. Not one stopped to ask if you were okay. Instead, they pulled on your gift. They needed the dancer, not the daughter. They needed the ministry, not the minister. They needed your performance, not your presence.

To them, your gift was useful.

But your pain was inconvenient.

This is where accountability in the church collapses—when the gift becomes more valuable than the person. When ministry becomes more about productivity than people. When leaders forget that the soul of the servant matters more than the service they provide.

Signs of Abuse Behind the Pulpit

You were manipulated into doing "ministry" their way instead of God's way.
Your time was taken for granted.
Your gift was prostituted.
Your boundaries were ignored.
Your obedience was exploited.
Your voice was silenced every time you spoke truth.

And the saddest part?
Everyone saw it.
No one addressed it.

They covered it up.
They normalized it.
They stayed silent.
They protected the system, not the sheep.

You even watched them allow a registered sexual offender to sit comfortably in the midst of the congregation and around children—completely unbothered, completely unchallenged. And when he began to prey on you, they still did nothing.

This wasn't church.
This was spiritual negligence wrapped in religious titles.

The Moment You Walked Away

On October 23, 2022, your pastor cussed three times in the pulpit while preaching. That was the moment your spirit said, No more. That was the moment the oil stopped flowing. That was the moment you knew God was releasing you from that house.

You stepped away from church, and from God, for almost two years.

But even in your distance, God stayed close.
Even in your silence, God whispered.
Even in your hurt, God healed.

And He brought you back, not through a church, but through assignment.
Not through religion, but through purpose.
Not through leadership, but through mentoring.

That was your turning point.
Not a building.
Not a service.
Not a sermon.
But a divine assignment that reminded you that heaven still had your name in its mouth.

A Prophetic Charge to Today's Preachers

To every preacher standing in a pulpit today:

If God called you, obey Him.
If you called yourself, sit down.

Stop bleeding on the people you're supposed to heal.
Stop preaching what you refuse to live.
Stop using the church as a business and the sheep as your income.
Stop preying on the weak and calling it ministry.
Stop hiding behind charisma and calling it anointing.

There was a time when Jesus overturned tables in the temple...
Trust me—there are some tables that need flipping again.

God's house is meant to be a place of prayer...
Not manipulation.
Not ego.
Not secret sin.
Not performance.
Not abuse.
Not idolatry.

A new generation is rising;
one that refuses to bow to religious foolishness,
one that discerns purity over performance,
one that honors character over charisma,
one that seeks God, not theatrics,
and one that is not afraid to say:

"Does the preacher believe what they preach?"

Chapter 2

When the Word Cuts Instead of Heals

There is a difference between being wounded for the Word and being wounded by the Word.

One produces growth.

The other produces confusion.

In the early years of my ministry journey, I assumed every sermon was born out of purity. I believed that every message was prayed through, lived through, and walked out before it was preached. I believed that spiritual leaders carried the weight of their words with sobriety and fear of the Lord.

But I quickly learned that not everyone who preaches the Word also submits to it.

I watched leaders stand behind the sacred desk declaring holiness, discipline, and surrender, only to walk away and live in direct contradiction to the very scriptures they proclaimed. I saw them shout about deliverance while privately wrestling with addictions they refused to confront. I heard them preach against sin while nurturing secret sins that were destroying them from within.

And as I sat there, hungry for truth and desperate for guidance, I found myself trying to reconcile their message with their lifestyle. How could someone preach so powerfully yet live so carelessly? How could they call others to holiness while refusing to walk in it themselves?

It wasn't the inconsistency that wounded me. It was the realization that their words were being used as a weapon, not a healing balm.

When Leadership Lives a Lie

I remember sitting in services where the atmosphere was charged, the music was high, and people were shouting all over the sanctuary. But even in the noise, my spirit could detect the impurity behind the performance. The sermons had sound but no substance. Fire but no foundation. Passion but no purity.

They were preaching messages they never intended to live. They were preaching to impress, not to transform. They were preaching from wounds they never acknowledged.

And when a leader refuses to heal, they end up preaching through their pain, bleeding on the very people they are called to lead.

It creates a cycle:

- The people imitate the preacher.

- The preacher imitates culture.

- And the church imitates chaos.

Somebody has to break that cycle.
Somebody has to speak up.
Somebody has to ask the hard question:
Does the preacher believe what they preach?

When the Word Is Used to Manipulate

I experienced moments where scripture was twisted—not for revelation, but for manipulation. Leaders used the Bible like a whip, not a guide. They used it to shame, silence, control, and guilt those who simply wanted to grow. They misquoted scripture to defend their preferences and ignored scripture that challenged their behavior.

The Word became a tool for obedience, not God's obedience, but theirs.

I saw leaders weaponize scripture to excuse their actions while condemning others for theirs. I heard sermons built around personal agendas instead of biblical truth. I felt the sting of being publicly corrected from the pulpit under the disguise of "rebuke," when the real motive was to humble me into submission.

It wasn't the scripture that hurt me.
It was the spirit behind it.

Anytime the Word of God is delivered without God's heart, it wounds instead of heals.

When Your Pain Becomes Inconvenient

There was a season when my soul was breaking—grief, disappointment, questions, spiritual exhaustion. And yet instead of compassion, I received pressure. Instead of support, I received expectation. Instead of love, I received silence.

Leaders wanted what I could *do*, not who I *was*.
They wanted ministry, not relationship.
They wanted gift, not authenticity.

My pain made them uncomfortable. My humanity made me a problem. And the moment my brokenness interfered with their agenda, I became disposable.

This is the wound that thousands carry silently in churches today, the wound of being needed but not nurtured. Valued for function but ignored in suffering.

The Weight of Being Betrayed by the Pulpit

There is no wound quite like the wound that comes from the person who taught you the Word.
You expect betrayal from the world.
You even expect it from friends.
But betrayal from the pulpit cuts the deepest.

Because leadership shapes belief systems.
Leadership molds faith.
Leadership is supposed to reflect the Shepherd, not replace Him.

But when leaders mishandle their call, the sheep begin to scatter.

It took me a long time to understand that it wasn't God who hurt me, it was people pretending to represent Him. People who used His name but didn't carry His heart. People who preached His Word but didn't live His truth.

And that realization is what began awakening my spirit to the difference between **church culture** and **Kingdom integrity**.

A Heart Cry in the Middle of Confusion

During the hardest parts of my journey, I found myself asking God questions I never thought I'd have to ask:

"Lord, how do I trust Your Word when the messenger is messy?"
"Father, how do I follow leaders who don't follow You?"
"God, how do I stay committed to ministry when ministry is where I was wounded?"

He didn't answer with rebuke.
He didn't shame me for questioning.
He met me with truth:

"Keep your eyes on Me. Leaders fail, but My Word stands."

It was the first time I realized the difference between loving the Word and loving those who preach it. It was the moment I understood that the messenger may fail, but the message never does.

What This Chapter Reveals

Chapter 2 is not about exposing people, it's about exposing systems and spiritual dysfunction that has gone unchecked for too long. It's about identifying the difference between a preacher who declares the Word and a preacher who embodies it.

Because at the end of the day:

A preacher who lives the Word will heal you.
A preacher who only quotes the Word will harm you.

And the question still echoes:

Does the preacher believe what they preach?

Chapter 3

The Making of a Spiritual Survivor

There are some lessons you can only learn by living through the fire. Not reading about it. Not hearing someone preach about it. Not watching someone else walk through it.

You have to feel it.
You have to survive it.
You have to come out on the other side with your soul still intact.

My journey in ministry didn't just expose broken systems, it trained my spirit. Every betrayal sharpened my discernment. Every disappointment developed my spiritual muscles. Every manipulation revealed what purity actually looks like. And every counterfeit leader taught me how to identify those who truly carry God's heart.

I didn't know it then, but I was being shaped, not destroyed.

When Your Anointing Attracts Warfare

Some people will never understand why you were attacked the way you were. They'll think you're being dramatic, sensitive, or emotional. But what they don't realize is this:

The enemy always fights what threatens him.

From the moment I stepped into leadership, I felt a level of warfare that didn't match my title, but it did match my calling. Spirits that sat comfortably in certain environments became agitated when I walked in. My obedience disrupted their agenda. My presence exposed their motives. My gift unsettled their comfort.

It took me a while to understand why certain leaders had an issue with me when I had done nothing wrong. But then God revealed:

"You don't fit their system because you don't belong to their system. You belong to Me."

I wasn't called to conform, I was called to confront.
I wasn't called to survive, I was called to see.
I wasn't called to blend in, I was called to break cycles.

And to do that, God had to train me in places where I would learn what corruption looks like up close.

Seeing Behind the Curtain

There is a moment in every believer's life when God pulls back the curtain. When He shows you what's really happening behind the scenes. When He reveals motives, intentions, and spirits that were operating under the disguise of ministry.

For me, it happened gradually, one encounter after another, until my eyes were fully opened.

I began to see:

- When preaching was performance instead of conviction

- When "glory" was emotional hype instead of true presence

- When leadership was built on ego instead of surrender

- When "protocol" was used to control instead of protect

- When gifts were exploited instead of nurtured

- When loyalty was demanded instead of mutually given

And once you can see, you can't unsee.
Your spirit refuses to go back to sleep.

Many people ask God for discernment, but they don't realize discernment is birthed in discomfort. It grows in deception. It sharpens in betrayal. It matures in environments where your spirit knows something is off even when your eyes can't yet identify it.

I didn't just survive dysfunction, I studied it. God made sure that when I eventually stepped into my true assignment, I would recognize what was holy and what was harmful.

This was survival training for my calling.

Understanding the Danger of Misusing a Gifted Vessel

Gifted people often receive the worst treatment in unhealthy churches, not because they're weak, but because they're powerful.

14

And the enemy knows it.
Leaders with impure motives know it.
And people who operate in the flesh instead of the Spirit know it too.

My gift wasn't nurtured; it was used.
My calling wasn't celebrated; it was drained.
My presence wasn't valued; it was exploited.

But hear me clearly:

God watches how His vessels are treated.

He doesn't take lightly when His daughters are mishandled.
He doesn't ignore it when His anointed ones are taken advantage of.
He doesn't overlook it when leaders use people for their own gain.

God allowed those seasons not to break me, but to build me.
I learned the hard way that my gift is not for hire, not for manipulation, and not for the agendas of men.
My gift belongs to God.
My anointing belongs to God.
My calling belongs to God.

And anyone who tries to misuse what God placed in me will eventually answer to Him.

Why Your Spirit Wouldn't Let You Settle

Even in my most discouraged seasons, when I walked away from the church, my spirit refused to let me settle. I tried to disconnect, but God kept pulling me back through purpose. I tried to hide, but purpose kept calling my name.

And that's the mark of someone truly chosen:

You can walk away from the building,
but the calling will never walk away from you.

My spirit was still alive.
My discernment was awakening.
My calling was maturing.
My endurance was being built.

What I saw as a breakdown turned out to be a breakthrough.

What I felt as abandonment revealed itself as alignment.

What I feared as rejection became a redirection.

God wasn't punishing me, He was promoting me. But before He could elevate me, He had to separate me… from people, systems, and spiritual environments that couldn't go where He was taking me.

The Survivor Becomes the Voice

One thing became clear:

I wasn't just surviving for myself; I was surviving for the ones coming behind me. For the ones who were too afraid to speak up. For the ones who thought they were crazy for seeing what others refused to acknowledge. For the ones sitting in pews questioning their sanity because the Word didn't match the behavior of the one preaching it.

I survived to speak the truth.

I survived to uncover deception.

I survived to guide others toward healing.

I survived so God could use me as a voice He could trust.

This chapter of my life wasn't about church hurt, it was about spiritual awakening.

A survivor doesn't come out immature.
A survivor comes out wiser.
Sharper.
More alert.
More equipped.
More surrendered.

And most importantly:
A survivor comes out with a calling that can no longer be intimidated by the foolishness of men.

Chapter 4

When Leadership Becomes Lordship

There is a thin line between leadership and lordship. A thin line between covering and control. A thin line between guidance and manipulation. And in many churches today, that line has not just been crossed; it has been erased.

I learned early on that some leaders don't want to shepherd; they want to dominate. They don't want to guide; they want to govern. They don't want to disciple; they want to dictate. Their goal isn't to raise up strong believers; it's to keep people dependent on them and their platform.

This is where spiritual abuse starts.
This is where deception grows.
This is where people begin to confuse the voice of their leader with the voice of God.

The Spirit Behind Control

Control doesn't always show up as yelling or force. Most times, it appears subtle. Soft. Spiritual. Scriptural.

It sounds like:

- "You need to obey your leader."

- "You're out of order."

- "Touch not my anointed."

- "You're rebellious for questioning me."

But underneath those phrases is a spirit that desires power, not purity.

I experienced it firsthand. Leadership wasn't pointing me toward God; they were pulling me toward themselves. I wasn't being spiritually covered, I was being spiritually confined. I wasn't being guided, I was being groomed to submit, conform, and obey without discernment.

This is not leadership.
This is lordship.

Anytime a leader wants authority without accountability, the flock becomes vulnerable. Anytime a leader uses fear or guilt to keep people connected, they're no longer shepherding, they're controlling.

And control is not of God. Control is the spirit of witchcraft dressed in religious attire.

The Misuse of the Word "Obedience"

One of the most dangerous weapons in church leadership is
the misinterpretation of obedience.
Obedience to God is holy.
Obedience to man is conditional.
But in abusive environments, the two become twisted together.

They used scripture to:

- Justify their demands

- Enforce their opinions

- Silence opposition

- Elevate their authority

- Mask their sin

- Keep people loyal

Obedience became less about the Holy Spirit and more
about hierarchy.

I heard leaders preach submission but live in secret sin.
I saw leaders demand honor they never earned.
I watched leaders discipline others for behavior they practiced
in private.

And when someone questioned the double standards,
suddenly they became "rebellious," "difficult," "out of order,"
or "ungrateful."

Truth became disrespect.
Discernment became disobedience.
Righteous confrontation became dishonor.

This is what happens when leadership turns into lordship; the truth becomes a threat to their system.

The Weapon of Silence

One of the most painful aspects of spiritual abuse is the silence of those who know better.

Leaders around them see the behavior.
Other ministers hear the conversations.
Congregants witness the actions.

But nobody speaks up.

They stay silent because:

- they're afraid

- they don't want to lose their position

- they don't want to become a target

- they don't want to be labeled "problematic"

- they think it's not their place

Silence becomes complicity.
Silence becomes protection for the abuser.
Silence becomes permission for the cycle to continue.

And for those being abused, silence becomes another wound.

I watched people see manipulation but pretend it wasn't happening. I watched them protect titles instead of souls. I watched them accommodate demons in leadership because "that's just how they are."

But God never called us to be loyal to dysfunction.

Any loyalty that requires silence about sin is not biblical, it's bondage.

When Leadership Lusts After Power—and People

One of the most dangerous mixtures in the church is a leader who desires authority but lacks integrity. When power is their appetite, the people become their prey. Emotional manipulation turns into spiritual seduction. Authority turns into entitlement. And the lines of holiness become blurred by private desires.

Some leaders don't want sons and daughters, they want access.
They don't seek accountability they crave admiration.

They don't honor covenant they desire control.

I experienced this kind of perversion firsthand; men in leadership using their titles to gain proximity, advantage, or private access to the women in the church.

This behavior isn't just immoral; it's demonic.
It destroys trust.
It distorts the image of God.
It leaves women wounded, intimidated, and spiritually violated.

Yet these same leaders stand behind pulpits every Sunday, preaching like God doesn't see everything they do.

Let me be clear:
God sees it. And God will judge it.

When You Break Free from Their Control

There comes a moment in every wounded believer's journey when God breaks the chains the church put on them. For me, it didn't happen through a deliverance line. It didn't happen through a prophetic word. It happened through revelation.

God opened my eyes and showed me that:

- Their approval wasn't necessary

- Their acceptance wasn't required

- Their oversight wasn't His covering

- Their system wasn't His Kingdom

- Their leadership wasn't His voice

The moment I realized that God had not called me to be ruled by man, something in me snapped free. The fear broke. The guilt lifted. The confusion cleared.

God began to teach me that no preacher, no bishop, no apostle, no prophet, no pastor should ever become the mediator between His voice and my destiny.

Jesus is Lord; not leadership.
Jesus is the Shepherd; not the ones wearing titles.
Jesus holds the church; not the ones who built the building.

The more God shook me free, the more I saw how deeply people were entangled in systems that were never ordained by Him. Systems designed to elevate leaders, not Christ.

Why God Allowed You to See the Darkness Up Close

There were times when I wondered why God allowed me to stay in environments that were clearly unhealthy. Why didn't He pull me out sooner? Why didn't He shield me from the harm? Why didn't He close the door before I walked into those places?

But with time, He revealed the truth:

"I allowed you to see it so you could expose it. I allowed you to experience it so you could heal others from it. I allowed you to walk through it so you would never become it."

God wasn't punishing me.

He was preparing me for what was ahead.

Preparing me to discern.
Preparing me to protect others.
Preparing me to preach truth, not tradition.
Preparing me to stand for holiness, not hypocrisy.
Preparing me to lead with compassion, not control.

And preparing me to boldly ask the question: **Do you believe what you preach? Or do you only preach what benefits you?**

Chapter 5

The Cost of Confronting Corruption

There comes a moment in every believer's journey when God requires them to stand. Not shout. Not dance. Not serve. Not perform.

But stand.

Stand in truth.
Stand in righteousness.
Stand in discernment.
Stand against the very thing that everyone else tolerates.

And the moment you choose truth over tradition, the cost becomes undeniable.

I learned early that confronting corruption in the church doesn't make you courageous in their eyes; it makes you a threat. It paints a target on you.. It exposes the places where leaders have become comfortable in compromise. And nothing agitates a corrupt system more than someone who refuses to bow.

They Only Loved You When You Were Silent

In unhealthy church systems, honor is rarely mutual; it's conditional.
As long as you:

- follow the rules

- never question the decisions

- stay loyal to dysfunction

- sacrifice yourself for the ministry

- serve without speaking

- obey without discernment

…they call you faithful.
They call you anointed.
They call you "submitted."

But the moment you speak up, everything changes.

When you pointed out the inconsistencies…
When you noticed the double standards…
When you began to see through the manipulation…
When you stopped allowing them to drain your gift…

Suddenly, you weren't "faithful" anymore; you were "rebellious."
You weren't "anointed"; you were "difficult."
You weren't "submitted"; you were "out of order."

They didn't want accountability.
They wanted agreement.
And the moment you stopped agreeing with the foolishness, the system turned on you.

The Retaliation of the Religious

Corrupted leadership doesn't confront truth; it attacks the one who speaks it.

The retaliation doesn't always look like open warfare. Sometimes it comes wrapped in spiritual language:

- Prayer meetings "about you" instead of with you

- Smear campaigns disguised as "concern"

- Leaders warning others to distance themselves

- Passive-aggressive sermons targeted at your character

- Suddenly losing opportunities you once freely operated in

- Your name being whispered instead of honored

The same people who celebrated you begin to avoid you.
The same leaders who once praised your gift begin to suppress it.
The same congregation that adored your ministry begins to question your motives.

Not because you sinned.
Not because you changed.
Not because you failed.

But because you spoke up.

Truth Always Exposes What People Want to Hide

When you have a discerning spirit, your very presence shines light on places others want to keep dark. Not because you're trying to uncover them, but because your spirit is awake. And when someone's influence depends on maintaining illusions, they cannot afford to let a person like you stay in the room.

So they isolate you.

They push you out quietly.
They make it uncomfortable for you to stay.
They whisper lies to protect their image.
They manipulate narratives to maintain power.

But what they didn't understand was this:

Removing you wasn't hindering you, it was releasing you.

Your exit was God's rescue mission.

Your separation was God's protection.

Your silence was God setting you up for clarity.

Your isolation was God's invitation into truth.

You didn't lose a church, you lost a trap.
You didn't lose a covering, you left a cage.
You didn't lose a leader, you survived a predator.

What they meant for harm, God was already turning into healing.

When Confrontation Costs You Your Community

One of the hardest losses isn't the loss of position, it's the loss of people.
People you loved.
People you served.
People you cried with.
People you ministered to.
People you danced with.
People you prayed for.

It hurts when the community you poured into more than anyone becomes the first community to withdraw from you.

It hurts when friends suddenly take sides.
It hurts when spiritual family becomes distant.
It hurts when those who knew the truth act like they never saw it.
It hurts when your character becomes a question and their behavior becomes excused.

But God taught me something powerful in that season:

Some people were never connected to your calling, they were connected to the comfort your presence gave them.

And when you confronted corruption, you disrupted their comfort.

You didn't lose people, you revealed them.
You didn't lose family, you uncovered alignment.
You didn't lose support, you discovered who never truly had your back.

This was not subtraction.
This was separation.

God Always Defends Those Who Stand for Righteousness

When I walked away from toxicity, I thought I walked away alone. But God began fighting battles I didn't even have the strength to pray about.
He vindicated quietly.
He exposed privately.
He protected strategically.
He healed intentionally.

Because when you stand for righteousness, heaven takes your case personally.

God showed me:

- Who was truly for me

- Who was using me

- Who was jealous of me

- Who was threatened by me

- Who was manipulating me

- Who was assigned to harm me

And then He removed them, one by one.
Not to punish them.
But to free me.

The more I confronted truth, the more God confronted what tried to break me.

The Cost Was High, But the Calling Was Higher

Confronting corruption cost me:

- A church family

- Mentors I trusted

- A community I loved

- Opportunities I served faithfully in

- Leadership positions I earned

- Friendships I thought were genuine

- A spiritual home I sacrificed for

But it also gave me:

- Clarity

- Discernment

- Strength

- Boundaries

- Authority

- Identity

- Purpose

- Freedom

And most of all, it gave me God in a deeper way.

He stripped away what people built so He could rebuild me Himself.

The cost was heavy.
But the calling was heavier.
And when I chose truth, heaven chose me.

Chapter 6

When God Becomes Your Only Pastor

There is a moment in every wounded believer's life when God steps in and says,

"Let Me pastor you."

Not the church.
Not leadership.
Not a personality.
Not a title.

Him.

When I walked away from the church, I felt disconnected from everything I knew; ministry, community, structure, routine, leadership, fellowship. It felt like I had left the only spiritual home I had ever known. But what I didn't realize was that stepping away from them was the only way I could step into Him.

God didn't meet me in a sanctuary; He met me in silence. He didn't restore me through a service; He restored me through stillness.

He didn't minister to me through a preacher; He ministered to me through presence.

This was the season where God Himself became my pastor.

The Shepherd Who Never Fails

Man had disappointed me.
Leadership had wounded me.
Church systems had drained me.
But the moment I stepped away, God began shepherding me personally.

He became:

- My covering when I had no covering

- My counselor when I had no one to talk to

- My comforter when I cried alone

- My guide when I didn't know where to go

- My teacher when the Word felt foreign

- My healer when nothing else worked

And the more I leaned into Him, the more I realized: **I had been dependent on men for what only God was ever supposed to provide.**

People had become my spiritual reference point, but God was reclaiming His position.

Learning to Hear God Again

After leaving the church, my spirit was scattered. I didn't trust sermons. I didn't trust leadership. I didn't trust ministry. And honestly… I didn't trust myself.

I questioned:

- "Was I wrong?"

- "Was I deceived?"

- "Did I miss God?"

- "Did I make a mistake?"

- "Who should I listen to now?

But God slowly rebuilt my spiritual confidence. He taught me how to hear His voice again; clearly, confidently, intimately.

Not through emotional hype.
Not through church noise.
Not through charisma.
But through quiet conviction.

He reminded me:

"My sheep recognize my voice and will not follow a stranger."

For the first time in a long time, I wasn't hearing God through a preacher; I was hearing Him directly. And that clarity began healing places I didn't even know were broken.

God Rebuilt My Identity Piece by Piece

Spiritual abuse doesn't just bruise the heart; it fractures identity. It makes you question your worth, your calling, your discernment, and your belonging.

But God began rebuilding me slowly:

- He restored my confidence

- He reminded me of my purpose

- He purified my gift

- He broke off guilt and shame

- He healed my spiritual vision

- He reintroduced me to myself

He reminded me of the woman He called before any church recognized me.
Before any leader affirmed me.
Before any title was placed on me.

God reintroduced me to the Meosha He ordained, not the one people shaped.

The Healing that Could Only Happen Outside the Church Walls

Sometimes God has to take you out of the environment that wounded you in order to heal you correctly. I learned this the hard way.

Healing didn't come from:

- sitting in another service

- attending another conference

- joining another ministry

- rushing back into another church

Healing came from:

- solitude

- honesty

- stillness

- tears

- therapy

- walking with God

- soul care

- time

This was the first time in my life where my healing wasn't rushed.
Where my gift wasn't demanded.
Where my presence wasn't pulled on.
Where my soul wasn't burdened.

I didn't have to dance.
I didn't have to serve.
I didn't have to perform.
I didn't have to pretend.

I could just… breathe.

Because when God is your pastor, rest becomes restoration, not rebellion.

When God Rebuilds Your Calling

One of the greatest miracles of this season was how God restored my calling. I thought ministry was over for me. I believed the damage ran too deep. I thought church trauma had disqualified me.

But God whispered,
"Your calling was never tied to a building. It was tied to Me."

And just like that, He began awakening what had been dormant:

- My ability to teach

- My discernment

- My prophetic sensitivity

- My compassion

- My love for the brokenhearted

- My boldness

- My voice

He didn't restore me so I could return to the same broken system.
He restored me so I could walk into what He originally assigned for me without filters, without limitations, without religious restrictions.

The Ministry That Was Born Out of Healing

When God became my pastor, He didn't just restore me, He prepared me.
Prepared me to minister to the wounded, the overlooked, the misused, the spiritually betrayed.

Prepared me to speak truth when others stay silent.
Prepared me to break cycles that have been normalized in

church culture.
Prepared me to stand boldly where others have bowed.
Prepared me to be a voice for the ones who are suffering in silence.

God didn't just heal me, He recalibrated me.

I didn't come out weaker.
I came out wiser.
Sharper.
More discerning.
More compassionate.
More aligned.
More surrendered.

And most importantly, I came out knowing the difference between a preacher and a pastor.

A preacher can inspire you.
A pastor can guide you.
Only God has the power to heal you.

Chapter 7

When Pain Turns Into Purpose

Pain has a way of feeling final.

It feels like the story is over like hope, desire, and calling have all come to an end.

But what I learned is this:

With God, pain is never the end, it's the beginning of purpose.

Every betrayal, every wound, every disappointment, every manipulation, every moment of spiritual abuse was not wasted. God took the very things the enemy used to break me, and He forged them into purpose.

Not just any purpose; a purpose with weight, authority, and oil.

Some purposes come from education.

Some come from training.

Some come from mentorship.

But the kind of purpose God placed on my life came through fire.

I didn't sign up for it.
I didn't choose it.
I didn't chase it.
But I survived it; and because I survived it, God entrusted me with it.

Brokenness Became My Birthplace

The seasons I thought would kill me were actually birthing me.
The betrayal that crushed me was actually molding me.
The silence that wounded me was actually developing me.
The manipulation that drained me was actually sharpening me.
The grief that overwhelmed me was actually deepening me.
The rejection that isolated me was actually positioning me.

I didn't realize it then, but God was turning my pain into a spiritual womb.
I wasn't being destroyed, I was being delivered into purpose.

Some purposes cannot be birthed on mountaintops, they are born in the wilderness.
Some callings cannot be carried in comfort, they are carried through suffering.
Some ministries cannot be taught, they must be lived.

Every tear watered the seed.
Every heartbreak fertilized the soil.
Every disappointment pruned me for fruitfulness.

Pain didn't disqualify me.
It prepared me.

Your Wounds Became Your Weapon

There's something powerful about a person who has been wounded but refuses to die.

A person who has been knocked down but refuses to stay down. A person who has been betrayed but refuses to become bitter.

Those are the people God can trust with real authority.

Your wounds became:

- a mirror for the broken

- a compass for the lost

- a warning for the naïve

- a voice for the silenced

- a weapon against deception

- a testimony of God's faithfulness

- a mantle for healing

- a foundation for your assignment

Nothing in your story was wasted.
Every wound became wisdom.
Every scar became strategy.
Every attack became insight.

God doesn't give authority to the unbroken, He gives authority to the healed.

The Ministry You Didn't Know You Were Becoming

Before you ever preached a sermon…
Before you ever wrote a book…
Before you ever ministered to a crowd…
You were already becoming the ministry.

Your life became the message.
Your survival became the sermon.
Your restoration became the revelation.
Your breakthrough became the blueprint.

God wasn't just preparing you to speak, He was preparing you to embody what you speak.

And because you lived through real warfare, you carry real oil.

People who have never suffered cannot lead the suffering. People who have never been wounded cannot heal the wounded.
People who have never survived deception cannot expose deception.

God allowed you to walk through the valley so He could build a ministry that carries power, not performance.

Purpose Arrived Quietly

Purpose doesn't always announce itself with trumpets and applause.
Sometimes it comes softly, like a whisper.

For you, it came through:

- a mentee who needed spiritual guidance

- a conversation that awakened your spiritual fire

- a moment where God reminded you, "I still see you"

- a stirring in your spirit that you couldn't shake

- a burden for the broken

- compassion for the wounded

- righteous anger toward spiritual abuse

- a desire to protect those who have been preyed upon

What you thought was a simple request from a former professor was actually God reintroducing you to your calling. You weren't just mentoring a student, you were stepping back into ministry.

Not the ministry that wounded you.
Not the ministry that used you.
Not the ministry that silenced you.

But the ministry God ordained for you from the beginning.

Your purpose didn't come from a pulpit.
It came from pain.
And because of that, it carries more authenticity and authority than anything you experienced in the church building.

Purpose Reveals Why Hell Fought You So Hard

When purpose begins to emerge, revelation follows: **Now I understand why I was attacked like that. Now I understand why the warfare was so intense. Now I understand why certain leaders targeted me. Now I understand why manipulation formed against me. Now I understand why I felt spiritually suffocated. Now I understand why God had to pull me out.**

You're not just another voice.

You're a *dangerous* voice.

You carry both testimony and truth.

Experience and discernment.

Compassion and conviction.

Hell doesn't fight the weak, hell fights the chosen.

Hell fights the called.

Hell fights the anointed.
Hell fights the ones who can set others free.

And now you see it.
Purpose wasn't birthed after the pain, it was birthed through it.

Chapter 8

The Voice God Gave Me

There are voices born from talent.
There are voices born from gifting.
There are voices born from charisma.
But then there are voices born from fire.

From survival.
From spiritual attack.
From betrayal.
From revelation.
From wilderness seasons.
From the breaking and remaking of the soul.

My voice was birthed in fire.

I am not who I am because someone laid hands on me. I am who I am because God laid His hand on me. And once He began shaping my voice, nothing, and no one, could silence it again.

A Voice That Sees What Others Overlook

People who sit in church pews every Sunday don't always see the spiritual systems functioning behind the scenes. But God gave me a unique lens. I don't just hear sermons, I discern spirits. I don't just watch services, I see motives. I don't just observe behavior, I recognize patterns.

My eyes opened in a way that could never be closed again.

I can spot:

- manipulation wrapped in spiritual language

- control disguised as "order"

- lust masquerading as "favor"

- emotional abuse packaged as "rebuke"

- ego dressed up as "authority"

- insecurity hiding behind the pulpit

- unhealed leaders functioning out of wounds

- ministry systems that protect titles but damage souls

What others call "discernment," I call survival instinct. It was developed in the fire of everything I lived through.

God didn't give me this voice to judge people; He gave me this voice to **protect His sheep**.

A Voice That Refuses to Bow to Titles

My experiences broke the fear of man off of me. I don't flinch at titles anymore. Apostle, bishop, prophet, pastor, evangelist; none of those intimidate my spirit. I honor God's order, but I don't worship people.

The fear of losing a position no longer controls me. The fear of being rejected no longer silences me. The fear of being misunderstood no longer stops me.

Because now I understand:

A title doesn't make you righteous; character does. A platform doesn't make you holy; your life does. A sermon doesn't make you anointed; your submission to God does.

God gave me a voice that is not impressed by eloquence or emotions.
I listen for authenticity.
I watch for humility.
I look for fruit.

If the life doesn't match the preaching, my spirit will never label it God.

That's the authority God built in me; an authority that cannot be manipulated by performance.

A Voice for the Wounded and Silenced

God didn't just give me a prophetic voice, He gave me a **protective** one.

A voice that carries empathy, compassion, and righteous indignation for those who have been:

- spiritually abused

- silenced

- used

- mishandled

- lied on

- exploited

- dismissed

- overlooked

- demonized for speaking truth

I carry them in my spirit.
I feel them deeply.
I see them even when nobody else does.

My mantle isn't just to speak, **it's to advocate**.

It's to uncover deception so the wounded can breathe again.
It's to challenge false systems so the oppressed can find freedom.
It's to expose manipulation so healing can begin.
It's to guide those who feel spiritually homeless back to the heart of God.

God trusted me with the ones who don't fit in church politics.
With the ones who see too much.
With the ones who feel too deeply.
With the ones who can't pretend anymore.

Those are the ones my voice reaches.

A Voice That Confronts What Others Fear

God gave me a boldness that I didn't ask for, a boldness that grew out of injustice and spiritual violation. A boldness that says:

"If it's wrong, I'm going to call it out."

"If it's manipulation, I'm going to expose it."

"If it's ungodly, I'm going to confront it."

"If it harms God's people, I will not be silent."

This boldness is not anger, it's assignment.

This boldness is not bitterness, it's clarity.

This boldness is not rebellion, it's responsibility.

This is why corrupt leaders dislike voices like mine:

I'm not afraid of losing access.

I'm not afraid of losing a seat.

I'm not afraid of losing connection.

I'm not afraid of losing favor.

When you've already been broken publicly, you lose the fear of standing boldly.

I am a danger to systems that thrive on silence… because my voice refuses to bow.

A Voice Refined by God, Not Religion

Everything God took me through purified my voice.

Every wound refined it.

Every betrayal deepened it.

Every season of isolation sharpened it.

My voice is not polished, it is purified.

Not trained by religion, trained by revelation.

Not molded by church systems, molded by the Holy Spirit.

Not rooted in tradition, rooted in truth.

God made sure my voice carried:

- authority without arrogance

- passion without performance

- conviction without cruelty

- empathy without enabling

- power without manipulation

- boldness without bitterness

- truth without theatrics

This is why people resonate with what I say; the voice was shaped in the wilderness, not the sanctuary.

A Voice God Trusts

This is the greatest honor of all:
God trusts my voice.

He trusts me to speak for the wounded.
He trusts me to correct with compassion.
He trusts me to confront with wisdom.
He trusts me to discern with clarity.
He trusts me to minister without manipulation.
He trusts me to love without bias.
He trusts me to protect His sheep with vigilance.

My voice is not just mine, it's an assignment.
It carries heaven's weight.
It carries heaven's burden.
It carries heaven's urgency.

And because of that, I cannot, and will not, be silent.

Chapter 9

Standing in the Calling God Meant for Me

There comes a moment in every believer's life when the fog clears, the confusion lifts, and the soul finally stands up straight again. Not timid. Not wounded. Not second-guessing.

But whole.
Rooted.
Clear.
Aligned.

This is the moment when the version of you God always intended steps forward and takes her rightful place.

I didn't get here overnight.
This version of me was carved, not created.
Shaped, not rushed.
Purified, not polished.
Refined, not rehearsed.

But standing on the other side of everything I survived, I can finally say:

I am walking in the calling God meant for me.

Not the calling others assigned to me.
Not the calling people tried to restrict me to.
Not the calling that required me to shrink, bow, or stay silent.
Not the calling dependent on approval, titles, or church politics.

But the calling birthed out of fire, revelation, and intimacy with God.

I Am No Longer Who I Was

The woman who endured manipulation is not the woman writing these words.
The woman who cried alone in ministry is not the woman speaking boldly now.
The woman who questioned her worth is not the woman standing in authority today.

I have evolved.

I became:

- stronger

- wiser

- clearer

- more discerning

- more compassionate

- more spiritually awakened

- more committed to truth

- more confident in God

- more confident in myself

The version of me who was once silenced now speaks with boldness.
The version of me who was ignored now moves with purpose.
The version of me who was wounded now ministers with power.

This is not the result of trauma, it is the result of transformation.

I Stand in an Authority That Cannot Be Taken

Man didn't give me this authority.
So man can't take it.
Ministry didn't give me this authority.
So ministry can't restrict it.
Leaders didn't activate this authority.
God did.

And because God gave it:

- it cannot be manipulated

- it cannot be negotiated

- it cannot be diminished

- it cannot be threatened

- it cannot be revoked

My authority was forged in the fires of what I lived through.
Not in a church program.
Not in a conference.

Not in a classroom.
In the battlefield of spiritual warfare and recovery.

This is what real authority looks like; authority that comes from survival, surrender, and submission to God.

I Stand in My Calling Without Apology

I no longer shrink to make others comfortable.
I no longer quiet my discernment to protect people's feelings.
I no longer hide my story to shield those who mishandled me.
I no longer question what God reveals, I trust it.
I no longer mute my prophetic voice, I release it.

I used to be afraid that speaking truth would make me look angry or rebellious.

Now I know that speaking truth makes me obedient.

My calling is not to be liked, it is to be effective.
My calling is not to fit in, it is to stand out.
My calling is not to be quiet, it is to sound the alarm.
My calling is not to maintain systems, it is to confront them.
My calling is not to entertain, it is to deliver.
My calling is not to follow religion, it is to follow God.

This is who I am now; unapologetically.

I Stand for the Wounded Because I Was Wounded

Some callings come from desire.
Some callings come from passion.
But the most powerful callings come from experience.

I stand for the spiritually wounded because I know what it feels like.
I protect those silenced by leadership because I was silenced.
I advocate for the misused because I was misused.

I expose deception because I lived through it.
I confront corruption because I survived it.
I guide the broken because I was broken.

God trusted me with the wounded because He healed me first.
Not partially.
Not superficially.
But deeply.

And because of that, my voice carries a weight that only comes from lived truth.

I Stand in a Ministry Born Out of Purity, Not Politics

My ministry is no longer tied to a building, denomination, or hierarchy.
My ministry is tied to God alone.

It is rooted in:

- truth

- healing

- clarity

- compassion

- deliverance

- discernment

- accountability

- integrity

- holiness

This is the ministry I was meant to carry.
This is the assignment God always intended.
This is the purpose birthed from everything I endured.

I'm not here to gather fans; I'm here to raise warriors.

I'm not here to keep people comfortable; I'm here to call them higher.

I'm not here to impress; I'm here to make an impact.

I'm not here to defend religion; I'm here to reveal God.

And God trusts me with this work because He knows I won't dilute it for approval.

I Stand in Obedience, Even When It Costs Me

Obedience is no longer optional.
It is my posture.
My lifestyle.
My commitment.

Even if it costs relationships.
Even if it costs acceptance.
Even if it costs comfort.
Even if it costs misunderstanding.
Even if it costs invitations.
Even if it costs platforms.

The only approval I seek now is God's.

Walking in this calling is not about being fearless, it's about being faithful.

And everything I lost in earlier seasons prepared me to obey God without hesitation in this one.

Chapter 10

A Call to Preachers; Live What You Preach

To every preacher, pastor, prophet, apostle, bishop, elder, leader, minister, or anyone who dares to stand behind a pulpit and declare the Word of God:

This is not an accusation.
This is not an attack.
This is truly an **invitation** and a **warning**.
A call to return to the heart of God and the holiness of His Word.

Because the truth is this:

We have more preachers than we have believers.
We have more sermons than we have substance.
We have more titles than we have truth.
We have more performances than we have purity.

And God is calling His leaders; loudly, urgently, and unmistakably, to return to **integrity, authenticity, humility, and obedience.**

This chapter is not just for them.
It is for any soul who has ever wondered:

Does the preacher truly believe what they preach?

The Pulpit Is Not a Stage, It Is an Altar

Too many pulpits have become platforms.
Too many sermons have become shows.
Too many leaders have become celebrities.
Too many churches have become businesses.

But the pulpit was never meant to be a stage. It was meant to be **an altar, a place where flesh dies and truth lives.**

When preachers treat the pulpit like a performance space, the people suffer.
The Word becomes diluted.
Conviction becomes optional.
Holiness becomes outdated.
And leadership becomes lordship.

God is calling His messengers to reclaim the pulpit as sacred ground.
Not a place to impress, but a place to repent.
Not a place to be seen, but a place to surrender.

Stop Preaching What You Will Not Practice

It is dangerous to preach what you do not live.
It is dangerous to declare what you will not obey.
It is dangerous to call people to holiness while living in hidden sin.
It is dangerous to demand surrender while refusing to bow yourself.

When a preacher's life contradicts their message:

- the anointing becomes contaminated

- the people become confused

- the church becomes divided

- the Spirit becomes grieved

- the enemy becomes emboldened

God is not impressed with charisma.
He is not moved by titles.
He is not persuaded by crowds.

He looks at the heart, and the heart always reveals the truth.

If you preach deliverance, live delivered.
If you preach holiness, live holy.
If you preach forgiveness, live forgiving.
If you preach purity, live pure.
If you preach faith, live faithfully.

God is not asking for perfection, He is demanding authenticity.

Stop Using the Word to Control and Manipulate

The Bible is not a weapon for manipulation.
It's not meant for dominance.

It's not meant to hide sin.
It is not an excuse for ego.
It's not an excuse for mistreatment.

It's not a shield for corrupt leaders.

When leaders twist scripture to:

- silence truth

- protect their reputation

- shame members

- exalt themselves

- excuse their behavior

- suppress accountability

They are not operating in anointing; they are operating in **witchcraft**, and using the Word to do it.

In God's eyes, this is an abomination.

Preachers, your words carry weight, but your heart carries more.
Your lifestyle speaks louder than your sermons.
Your hidden character speaks louder than your public ministry.

Return to Holiness Before You Return to the Pulpit

Holiness is not old-fashioned.
Holiness is not legalism.
Holiness is not optional.

Holiness is the mark of a true messenger.

This generation does not need:

- louder preachers

- more emotional sermons

- bigger platforms

- flashier ministries

This generation needs **holy leaders**.
Leaders who walk what they preach.
Leaders who tremble at the Word of God.
Leaders who live with integrity even when no one is watching.
Leaders who repent quickly.
Leaders who are accountable.
Leaders who are humble.
Leaders who prioritize soul care over stage presence.

Preachers, God is not asking for your performance. He is asking for your purity.

If God Called You, Obey Him.

If You Called Yourself, Sit Down.

This is the hardest truth, but the most necessary:

Not every preacher standing in a pulpit was placed there by God.

Some were placed there by:

- ambition

- insecurity

- ego

- church politics

- tradition

- self-appointment

- opportunism

If God did not call you, step aside before you cause more harm.
If God did call you, rise up and obey Him fully.

Because the ones who walk in obedience look different.
Their spirit is different.
Their posture is different.
Their fruit is different.

You cannot fake God's calling; you can only fake it until the truth exposes you.

And God does not bless impostors, He exposes them.

Your Words Have Power; Use Them Carefully

Every preacher carries the weight of influence.

Your words can:

- heal or wound

- free or bind

- uplift or destroy

- guide or confuse

- nourish or drain

Preaching is not just speaking; it is spiritual assignment.
It is responsibility.
It is stewardship.
It is leadership.
It is accountability before God.

If your words do not match your life, heaven keeps the record.
Be careful what you preach.
Be careful how you live.
Be careful whose soul you're shaping.

God holds leaders to a higher standard for a reason.

A Prophetic Charge to This Generation of Preachers

God is raising a remnant of leaders who:

- fear God more than they fear losing members

- prioritize purity over popularity

- preach truth even when it's not convenient

- live holy even when no one is watching

- love people rather than use them

- rest rather than perform

- walk in integrity rather than manipulation

He is shaking pulpits.
He is exposing false leadership.
He is dismantling religious kingdoms built on ego.
He is purifying the Bride of Christ.

And He is calling preachers back to the place where their sermon and their life match.

Not perfection, but alignment.

Not charisma, but character.

Not hype, but holiness.

Not entertainment, but obedience.

Not performance, but purity.

The Final Question That Matters Most

As this book closes, the question that started it now echoes with deeper weight:

Preacher, do you believe what you preach?
Do you live it?
Do you honor it?
Do you walk it out?
Do you submit to it?
Do you obey it?
Do you fear God enough to practice what you declare?

Because at the end of the day:

Your sermon may touch people, but your life will transform them.

And God is calling His leaders to live what they preach.

Starting now.

CONCLUSION

Stepping Into Truth, Healing, and Alignment

As you reach the end of this book, I pray you feel something shifting inside you; a settling, a clarity, a breath you didn't realize you were holding. These pages were never written to reopen wounds, but to *reveal the truth hiding beneath them*. They were not written to tear down the Church, but to cleanse her; beginning with the hearts of those who have been silently hurting.

If you recognized yourself in these pages, know this: **You're not crazy. You're not overreacting. You're not being rebellious. You're not alone.**

You are a believer who saw something that did not align with God's heart, and your spirit responded accordingly.

Your discernment was not a problem.
Your questions were not a lack of faith.
Your pain was valid.
And your journey matters.

What you walked through does not disqualify you.
It does not stain your calling.
It does not diminish your purpose.

Instead, it has *equipped* someone like you.
It has strengthened your voice.
It has deepened your compassion.

It has sharpened your discernment.
It has brought you into alignment with God, not religion.

You survived what others never talk about.
You endured what many pretend does not happen.
You kept walking when your spirit was weary.
You kept believing when your heart was broken.

And whether you realize it yet or not, God is pleased with you.

Not because you were perfect.
But because you were honest.
Because you kept searching for Him even when people misrepresented Him.
Because you chose healing over hardness.
Because you chose truth over silence.
Because you chose God over the systems built around Him.

This book was never meant to be the end of your story, it is the threshold into your next season. A season of:

- clarity after confusion

- peace after chaos

- healing after hurt

- purpose after pain

- strength after survival

- truth after trauma

- intimacy after isolation

A season where God Himself becomes your guide, your voice, your reassurance, your covering, your pastor, and your peace.

As you close this book, I encourage you to walk forward with boldness and freedom.

Release whatever no longer aligns with God's truth. Forgive what you can, surrender what you can't, and trust God with every part of your story.

And if you are called to lead, if there is ministry inside of you, let this book be your reminder:

Live what you preach.
Love who you lead.
Guard your heart.
Remain accountable.
Stay humble.
Walk in integrity.
And let your life, not your sermons, be the truest evidence of your calling.

May the God who healed me heal you.
May the God who found me find you.
May the God who restored me restore you.
And may the God who gave me my voice give you yours.

This is not the end.

This is your awakening.

This is your moment of clarity.

This is the turning point in your life.

This is your invitation back into alignment with the One who never left you.

May you walk forward whole, discerning, empowered, and anchored in truth.

The God who comforts the wounded is with you.

The God who speaks to the silenced is speaking to you now.
And the God of restoration is leading you home.

CLOSING PRAYER

A Prayer of Healing, Clarity, and Holy Alignment

Father, in the name of Jesus,
I lift up every person who has walked through these pages.
Every heart that has carried silent wounds.
Every mind that has wrestled with confusion.
Every soul that has suffered under leadership that did not
reflect You.
Every believer who has questioned their faith because of what
they experienced in the church.

Lord, I thank You for seeing them.
You know them.
You understand them.
You have never abandoned them; not for one moment.
And today, I ask that You wrap them in Your presence in a
way that cannot be denied.

God, heal the places that were broken by spiritual authority.
Restore the places that religion tried to silence.
Rebuild the parts of them that were damaged by people who
carried Your name but not Your heart.
Remove every residue of manipulation, control, shame, guilt,
fear, and confusion.
Lift the weight of disappointment.
Lift the weight of betrayal.

Lift the weight of unanswered questions.
And replace it with Your peace; the peace that surpasses all understanding.

    Father, purify their discernment.
Sharpen their spiritual ears.
Awaken their spiritual eyes.
Give them clarity where there was once doubt.
Give them confidence where there was once hesitation.
Give them boldness where there was once fear.
And give them rest where there was once exhaustion.

Lord, remind them that their relationship with You was never meant to be filtered through flawed humanity.
You are their Shepherd.

You are their covering.

You are their comfort and guide.

You are their healer.

And You are the One who restores their soul...

I speak a divine reset over their spirit;
a reset of identity,
a reset of calling,
a reset of faith,
a reset of trust,
a reset of purpose.

    Let every place that was wounded become a well of wisdom.
Let every place that was broken become a place of breakthrough.
Let every painful memory become proof of Your keeping power.
Let every tear become a testimony.

And Father, I pray for leaders as well.
For the preachers, pastors, prophets, and teachers who hold
Your Word.
Call them to return to purity.

Call them to return to humility.

Call them to return to accountability.

Call them to return to Your heart.
Remove the theatrics.
Strip away the ego.
Burn up the pride.
And let conviction lead them back to holiness.

Raise up a generation of leaders who mean what they
preach and live what they declare.
Leaders who tremble at Your Word.
Leaders who walk in integrity.
Leaders who carry compassion.
Leaders who heal and don't harm.
Leaders who shepherd and don't control.
Leaders who serve and don't dominate.
Leaders who reflect You, not themselves.

God, seal this work in the hearts of every reader.
Let not one seed be stolen.
Let not one revelation be choked out.
Let not one healing be reversed.
Cover them with Your blood.
Cover them with Your truth.
Cover them with Your grace.
Cover them with Your presence.

And as they close this book,
let them open a new chapter in You.

A chapter of freedom.
A chapter of clarity.
A chapter of wholeness.
A chapter of boldness.
A chapter of purpose.
A chapter of renewed relationship with You.

Father, I declare that they will walk in truth.
They will walk in discernment.
They will walk in healing.
They will walk in identity.
They will walk in power.
They will walk in purity.
They will walk in You.

In Jesus 'mighty name,
Amen.

ABOUT THE AUTHOR

Meosha Culpepper is a minister, author, soul care advocate, and prophetic voice called to bring healing, clarity, and restoration to those wounded within the walls of the church. With a deep passion for truth and spiritual integrity, she boldly addresses the often-unspoken realities of spiritual manipulation, leadership hypocrisy, and the misuse of power disguised as ministry.

A servant leader at heart, Meosha equips individuals to reconnect with God beyond religious performance, rediscover their identity, and walk boldly in the calling God intended for them. Her journey through spiritual betrayal and spiritual restoration has shaped her into a champion for the overlooked, the silenced, and the spiritually displaced.

Meosha is also the founder of **TER Ministries**, where she empowers caregivers, leaders, and those battling burnout to find renewal through faith, self-care, and soul restoration. Her work extends to retreats, mentorship, coaching, and publishing support for emerging authors who desire to share their stories.

Known for her transparency, compassion, and prophetic discernment, Meosha uses her voice to uncover truth, heal wounds, and guide God's people back to alignment with Him. Her message is bold, uncompromising, and rooted in love; reflecting a life touched, refined, and led by God.

Meosha Culpepper

Meosha resides in Texas, where she continues to write, serve, minister, and mentor others on their journey toward emotional, spiritual, and relational wholeness.

74

CONNECT WITH THE AUTHOR

Thank you for reading Does the Preacher Believe What They Preach?
If this book has spoken to your heart, encouraged your healing, or awakened your clarity, Meosha would love to stay connected with you.

Stay connected, stay encouraged, and stay aligned.

Website

https://terministries.com
(A central hub for books, ministry updates, retreats, speaking engagements, and soul care resources.)

Email

info@terministries.com
For prayer requests, mentorship inquiries, collaborations, and speaking invitations.

Social Media

Facebook: *https://www.facebook.com/terministries/*
Instagram: *https://www.instagram.com/terministries/*
LinkedIn: *https://www.linkedin.com/in/meosha-culpepper-6425312b/*
YouTube: *https://www.youtube.com/@terministriesInc*

Speaking & Ministry Requests

Meosha is available for:

- Church engagements

- Women's conferences

- Healing and deliverance gatherings

- Soul care workshops

- Caregiver support events

- Author panels & writing workshops

- Leadership accountability conversations

To invite Meosha to your event, please schedule a meeting on her calendar:
https://link.theomnisuite.com/widget/bookings/meosha-calendar

Join the Community

Stay tuned for:

- New book releases

- Workshops

- Bible studies

- Online healing circles

- Retreats

- Soul care programs

- Author coaching opportunities

Your journey toward wholeness is sacred. Meosha looks forward to walking with you as God continues to restore, awaken, and empower your life.

GROUP DISCUSSION PROMPTS

For Bible studies, circles, or retreats

- **"Where do we see wounded believers today, and how can we become part of their healing?"**

- **"What does accountability look like when the leader is the one out of alignment?"**

- **"How do we differentiate between conviction from God and control from man?"**

- **"What would a healthy, healed leadership culture look like in today's church?"**

- **"How do we protect the next generation from spiritual abuse?"**

PERSONAL DECLARATIONS FOR HEALING

- I am no longer silenced — my voice belongs to God.

- My discernment is a gift, not a burden.

- I release every wound that tried to reshape my identity.

- I choose healing, clarity, and truth.

- I walk with God, not the expectations of man.

- I trust the God who saw every moment and still calls me whole.

- I will not confuse the failures of leadership with the character of God.

- I step into alignment, boldness, and purpose — unapologetically.

Publisher Imprint Information

BUT GOD Publishings LLC

"Where Testimonies Become Truth, and Stories Become Seeds."

BUT GOD Publishings LLC is an independent, faith-centered publishing imprint founded by Meosha Culpepper. The imprint is dedicated to amplifying powerful stories of healing, faith, identity, and spiritual transformation. With a mission to elevate voices that carry truth and inspire wholeness, BUT GOD Publishings produces books that restore hope, awaken purpose, and guide readers back to the heart of God.

BUT GOD Publishings LLC publishes works focused on:

- Faith-based empowerment

- Spiritual healing

- Soul care and restoration

- Emotional and mental wellness

- Testimony-driven transformation

- Ministry, leadership, and accountability

- Christian living and personal growth

Each project is crafted with excellence, integrity, and prayer, reflecting the belief that every story assigned by God deserves to be told with purity and power.

Publisher:
BUT GOD Publishings LLC
Pflugerville, Texas

Website: butgodpublishings.com
For submissions, collaborations, or inquiries:
butgodpublishings@gmail.com